PINEAPPLE PODCASTING

SAMANTHA LEE WRIGHT

PINEAPPLE PODCASTING

The Ultimate Beginner's Guide to Creating, Launching, and Monetizing a Podcast, with Zero Experience and a Shoestring Budget

Book and Cover Design by Maya Roman

For information about permission to reproduce selections from this book, contact sam@samanthaleewright.com with "Permissions" in the subject line. For information about speaking engagements or podcast coaching, contact sam@samanthaleewright.com

Published in the United States of America.

ISBN 9798558939408

November 2020

Dedication

To my husband Shamba, kids August and Layla, and my twin sister Michelle, without whom this book would not exist. I love you with all my heart and then some.

TABLE OF CONTENTS

INTRODUCTION

SECTION I WHY PODCAST

A Brief History of Podcasting 13

The Advantages of Podcasting 17

SECTION II HARNESSING YOUR IDEA

How to Stand Out 23

What's in a Name? 27

SECTION III BRINGING YOUR IDEA TO LIFE

Podcasting Equipment 35

Ready, Set, Record! 41

Tips For Conducting Great Interviews 49

Podcast Editing 53

Last But Not Least 59

SECTION IV LAUNCHING

Consistency is King 69

Media Host 71

Launch Strategies 75

SECTION V MONETIZING

How to Make Money in Podcasting 89

CONCLUSION

A Pineapple Podcaster 101

Stand Tall
WEAR A CROWN
& Be Sweet
ON THE iNSiDE

INTRODUCTION

Over 10 million hours of content gets published to YouTube each month. There are roughly 30 million active blogs on the internet today. And a whopping 1.5 billion daily active users are on Facebook. When it comes to standing out in the online world, the competition is high!

Compare this, however, to the world of podcasting. In 2020, at the time of this writing, there are roughly 750,000 active podcasts on iTunes. And while that's nothing to sneeze at, it goes to show that in the world of podcasting, there's still plenty of room for creatives to make their mark.

I'm here to help you create a podcast that stands out from those other shows — the way a pineapple stands out in a sea of bland, boring fruits in the produce aisle. We're going to make your show the pineapple of podcasts — unique, yet massively appealing, and sweet to listen to. Throughout the journey of this book, you will learn how to get your podcast noticed, grow a following, and have a good time doing it.

You will learn not to settle for boring and hold yourself and your show to a higher standard. You will prioritize great sound quality, show up consistently, and be smart about your content. You will be strategic about launching, growing, and monetizing your podcast, and you'll do it all with a bootstrap mentality that doesn't let a lack of funds or know-how hold you back.

When I started my podcasting journey in 2015 I was a stay-at-home mom of two small children, running a part-time business, and had no clue what I was getting myself into. I had no funds for fancy equipment or any sort of podcast "how-to" course. What I did have was a laptop, the internet, and a message to share with the world. In December 2015, after only three months of research and planning, I launched my very own podcast, *The Essential Oil Revolution.*

Now, over 3.5 million downloads later, I have turned my podcast into a global brand. I earn a steady income that supports my family, and I maintain the #1 rating for essential oil podcasts in the world.

My hope is that this book helps you achieve your own success. I want it to help bring your ideas and passions to life, resulting in something new and exciting for you and for the world of podcasting. I want you to reach your financial goals and become a prominent voice in your field.

I want you, my friend, to become.... a Pineapple Podcaster.

xo,

Samantha Lee Wright

"THE TONGUE
CAN PAINT WHAT
THE EYES CAN'T SEE."

– CHINESE PROVERB

SECTION I
WHY PODCAST

A BRIEF HISTORY OF PODCASTING

"For the last year, I've spent every working day trying to figure out where a high school kid was for an hour after school one day in 1999— or if you want to get technical about it, and apparently I do, where a high school kid was for 21 minutes after school one day in 1999. This search sometimes feels undignified on my part. I've had to ask about teenagers' sex lives, where, how often, with whom, about notes they passed in class, about their drug habits, their relationships with their parents. And I'm not a detective or a private investigator. I've not even a crime reporter. But, yes, every day this year, I've tried to figure out the alibi of a 17-year-old boy."

How's *that* for an intro?

This opening, read by Sarah Koenig (creator of the 2012 award-winning podcast *Serial)*, had millions of listeners hooked instantly. Everyone was dying to hear the story and binging their way to find out...guilty or not guilty.

"Do you listen to *Serial*?" became the conversation starter of the decade. Countless references were seen in popular culture. Celebrities like Ewan McGregor, Sarah Silverman, Rashida Jones, and Brie Larson, were all talking about whether or not Adnan Syed was guilty of murder.

Serial was one of the first ever binge-worthy and share-worthy podcasts to hit the public eye. Its contribution in pushing podcasts into the cultural mainstream was undeniable, and in 2015 it became the first podcast ever to win a Peabody award.

P.S. If you loved Serial, be sure to check out the podcast *Undisclosed* to travel further down the rabbit hole of Adnan Syed's case.

After listening to *Serial*, many listeners finally began exploring their podcast apps, which had been sitting preinstalled on their phones for years without notice. Creative and insightful shows like *Radiolab, This American Life,* and *Reply All* proved to the masses that podcasts were a brilliant new form of media that could be enjoyed on-demand, for free, right from their phone or computer.

It took a show like *Serial* to popularize podcasts as we know them today, but they'd been making headway since the technology's inception in 2004. Dave Winer is credited with the invention of podcasting by helping create the web-feed technology that makes distributing audio content via the internet possible. He launched what is considered by many to be the first ever podcast, *Morning Coffee Notes*, on August 12th, 2004. However, it is Adam Curry, a former MTV video jockey who is credited as the Godfather of podcasting (or "Podfather") by popularizing the platform with his hit show *Daily Source Code*. In 2005, early shows like Leo Leporte's *This Week In Tech* and Gretchen Vogelzang & Paige Heninger's *Mommycast* began making ground and growing in popularity.

In June 2005, Apple iTunes 4.9 released with a native support function for podcasts and in January 2006, Steve Jobs demonstrated how to make a podcast as his keynote presentation at Macworld. In 2007 Ricky Gervais set a Guinness World Record for the most downloaded podcast, reaching 261,670 downloads per episode in his first month of launching *The Ricky Gervais Show*. Just 4 years later, the *Adam Corolla Show* shattered records by reaching over 59 million unique downloads after 3 years of podcasting.

Surpassing all expectations, in 2011, Apple reported reaching over 1 billion podcasts subscribers. And today, more Americans listen to podcasts than attend church each week. Talk about growth!

LOOKING AHEAD

The history of podcasting is one of rapid change and steady growth, and by the time you read this book, new developments will already have taken hold. One of the most significant developments at the time of this writing is the release of the first ever large-scale podcasting subscription platform called Luminary—the self-proclaimed "Netflix of podcasting." This app charges consumers to listen to podcasts, and in return they receive ad-free content and access to shows not found anywhere else.

Prior to Luminary's aggressive launch campaign in early 2019, the podcasting landscape had been one of mainly independent creators and free media distribution. But Luminary, armed with millions of dollars in venture capital, was the first to launch a podcast app that charges a monthly fee to listeners ($4.99/mo currently— a significant decrease from its original $8/mo launch price).

The effects of subscription-based podcast distribution have not gone unnoticed, especially by podcast fans who have suddenly had their favorite shows become unavailable and guarded behind a monthly paywall. Time will tell how Luminary's platform will impact the podcast industry, but for now, let's focus on the awesome truth: podcast aren't going anywhere.

THE ADVANTAGES OF PODCASTING

Podcasts have several unique characteristics that make them the perfect platform for creatives to share their ideas with the world.

ADVANTAGE #1: ON-DEMAND LISTENING

Unlike radio, where you have to tune into your favorite programs at specific days and times, podcasts are available 24/7, so you can listen whenever and wherever, so long as you have a phone or computer.

The idea that people were once at the beck and call of their radio programmers seems absurd now. That may have worked for families in the 1930s, all huddled around their radios for FDR's *Fireside Chats*, but in today's on-demand society (Netflix, Hulu, Amazon, etc.) people are opting to read, listen, and watch what they want, when they want it — and podcasts give them just that.

ADVANTAGE #2: PORTABLE

One of the greatest advantages of podcasts is that they can be streamed or downloaded very easily. Because their file sizes are much smaller compared to most video content, even users with slow internet, or bad cell service can usually manage to stream an episode. When downloaded in advance, listeners can tune-in to their favorite shows on a plane, while hiking, or wherever life may take them. This portability gives you, the podcaster, a huge advantage when it comes to reaching consumers.

ADVANTAGE #3: MULTITASK-ABLE

Unlike video, or written media, podcast listeners can have their eyes and hands free while enjoying content. This multitask-able trait is a huge reason why people are so addicted to podcasts. Countless listeners have told me that my voice keeps them company on their drive to work, dog walks, or during meal prep. As a podcaster, you can offer value to people without taking time away from their daily tasks. And there's nothing people value more than their time!

ADVANTAGE #4: QUICKLY BUILDS INTIMACY

According to Emma Rodero, a communications professor at the Pompeu Fabra University in Barcelona, "Audio is one of the most intimate forms of media because you are constantly building your own images of the story in your mind and you're creating your own production...something that you can never get with visual media."

Hearing someone's voice creates a level of intimacy that reading simply cannot touch, save for the most gifted of authors. Also, perk for you — you get to go to work in your PJs!

ADVANTAGE #5: ACCESSIBILITY (AKA POWER TO THE PEOPLE!)

Unlike the film, radio, or television industries, podcasting is extremely accessible for creators. The low cost of producing and distributing a podcast basically means that anyone with a laptop and $50-$200 can think of an idea, craft that idea into a podcast, and put it out into the world for all to hear.

The cost of starting a podcast will vary, of course, depending on the size of the project. Big shows like *This American Life* or *In the Dark*, which have large staffs and do intensive investigative reporting, may spend hundreds of thousands of dollars on just one episode of their show. While, *Sleep With Me Podcast* — a twice-weekly show so boring it puts you to sleep (on purpose) probably cost about $300 to launch. This quirky podcast was one of Esquire's "Top 25 Essential Podcasts of 2016," which goes to show that no matter the budget, a podcast can generate record downloads and impressive profits.

The ability to bring your vision to life is in your hands. With just a few basic tech skills and some minor equipment, you can share your message with the world. So come along Pineapple Podcaster, let's get you going!

"THEY LAUGH
AT ME BECAUSE I'M
DIFFERENT; I LAUGH AT
THEM BECAUSE THEY'RE
ALL THE SAME."

- KURT COBAIN

SECTION II
HARNESSING YOUR IDEA

HOW TO STAND OUT

Before diving into the how, let's talk about the what. What is your podcast going to be about? How will your podcast stand out amongst the crowd? Will you be just another regular Joe, interviewing your "smart friends," and editing down hours of incessant rambling? Or will you bring something of value?

Heaven knows, the last thing the world needs is another mediocre podcast with a couple of dudes sitting on a couch, talking and cursing over each other amidst a noisy background. What the world does need is YOU.

Whether your podcast nourishes people through humor, knowledge, entertainment, a new perspective, or just a connection to the human race, my plea to you is that you create something that serves others and leaves you feeling proud.

If you already have an idea for a show, take some time to research what's already out there in your chosen genre. Dig deep and investigate so that you know how to set your show apart. Will you showcase minorities, talk about taboos, make your show significantly longer or shorter than the standard 20-60 mins, or use interesting sound techniques? I've seen new shows fly past their competition simply by investing the time and energy into getting better sound quality!

How will your show stand out?

WHAT YOUR PODCAST IS ABOUT

Think for a moment about the different kinds of shows that exist on TV today. There are news channels, political shows, sitcoms, game shows, pre-teen, sci-fi, history, and more.

Podcasting is no different! There are podcasts for kids, for adults, and for every type of person you can think of. There are niche podcasts about poker, food trucks, fashion and parenting. And there are fictional, episodic podcasts similar to your favorite TV shows.

Podcasting is not defined by rules, guidelines, formats, or standards. They can be created by celebrities, big brands, and networks, or by the middle-schooler down the street for a school project.

If you need to get your brainstorm juices flowing, check out some of these successful and unique shows:

- **Everything is Alive** - A podcast that interviews inanimate objects such as a subway bench or balloon (it's weird and hysterical).
- **Welcome To Night Vale** - Presented as a radio show for a fictional town called Night Vale. Listen to the bizarre and eerie reporting of the strange events that occur.
- **FoodTruckr School** - Learn how to start, run, and grow a

successful food truck business.

- **Tai Asks Why** - 11 year old Tai investigates life's big questions such as "Why is space so dark," "What is love," and "What is fear and why are we born with it?"
- **Dan Carlin's Hardcore History** - 3 - 6 hour-long history lessons that hold nothing back.
- **Up and Vanished** - A novice documentarian uncovers some unexpected mysteries surrounding the disappearance of a small town's beloved beauty queen.
- **Girl Tales** - Traditional fairytales rewritten to empower the female characters and highlight current social issues. For example, in "The Literate Mermaid" Myra solves the problem of trying to read her books without having them destroyed by ocean water.

When crafting your show idea, take time to think through the following questions. Trust me, getting clear on these answers is *necessary* for success:

Who is your show for?

Is your show made for kids, baby boomers, bachelors, or brides-to-be? Take any course on podcasting and the first thing they'll ask is, "Who will listen?" Entrepreneurs, LGBTQ+, parents, musicians? What combinations of demographics will make up your audience?

Why will people listen?

Will they listen in the hopes to laugh, to learn, to cry, to feel connected, to pass the time, to earn money, to lose weight, or to master the art of grammar? When I started *The Essential Oil Revolution*, I wanted to create something for people itching to learn the what, why, and how of essential oils. My vision was clear from the start. And while the choices and endless possibilities may seem overwhelming to you, just know this: the only hard and fast rule of Pineapple Podcasting is — make your podcast something that excites you!

Action Step
Write down your podcast idea/s. Then answer these questions:

- ▷ Who will listen and how will they benefit?
- ▷ How will your show be different than what's out there already?
- ▷ How much does your idea excite you?

WHAT'S IN A NAME?

Choosing your show's name is a very important task. Obviously, you want your name to indicate what your show is about, but you also want it to be a name that you like and sounds interesting.

If you are starting out from scratch (as in, you don't have an audience or contract with an established production company), then you will want your podcast title to include keywords that optimize your search results. This may result in a slightly less cool or clever sounding show name, but trust me, keywords trump cleverness when it comes to starting a podcast from scratch.

For example, when I started my show, I was a big fat nobody. There were several shows already on the topic of essential oils, and I needed to maximize every advantage I could think of to get my show on the map. My show is for a very niche audience. As a rule of thumb, niche topics should include keywords in the title of their show. I knew I wanted my podcast to show up for people searching the term "essential oils" in their podcast app. Therefore, I deliberately put the words "Essential Oil" in my title. My show is called "*The Essential Oil Revolution*" for a deliberate reason: search engine optimization!

If I had named my show *"Lemon & Lime," "Drops of Joy," "Smell the Roses," "Unicorn Tears,"* or *"Sam Loves Lavender,"* I can guarantee you I would not be where I am today. From very early on I could say with confidence; "Search for 'essential oils' in any podcast app and my show will be the first thing you see."

This was only possible because I used important keywords in my title. Sure, I would have loved to have a shorter, snappier, wittier podcast name, but being findable was more important to my goals than sounding cool.

iTunes and other podcast apps place much more importance on your show title versus your show description when it comes to the algorithm that determines which podcasts show up in search results. Therefore, if you have a niche or targeted podcast concept, be sure to include one or two keywords in your show title whenever possible. Have a show about gardening? Include the word "gardening" in the title. Have a show about crafts and sewing? Include the words "craft and sew" in your title. Using keywords to your advantage will make you grow faster! I promise.

KEYWORD STUFFING

iTunes used to allow for long show titles and brackets. This helped a lot with what's known as keyword stuffing. For example, in the beginning, my official show name according to the iTunes database was *"The Essential Oil Revolution | Aromatherapy and Natural Living Herbal Education."* This allowed me to include more keywords in my title for people searching terms like "aromatherapy," or "natural," or "herbs" in their podcast apps. However, iTunes is starting to deny show names based on keyword stuffing. Keep this in mind, but don't shy away from experimenting with what you can get away with. You may have to resubmit your show title if it gets denied, but it's worth the try. For more information on this topic, check out episode 334 of *The Audacity to Podcast*.

So, while you may be tempted to give your Scrabble themed podcast a clever sounding name like "Tile Talk" instead of "Scrabble Strategies," keep in mind that if you want to grow an audience from scratch, you need to be findable, and to do that you need to prioritize using keywords in your show title. If you love your show title idea and it doesn't include keywords, try including them after a bracket or dash and see if iTunes will allow for it. For example, try making your official show title "Tile Talk - For Scrabble Lovers," and see if it gets accepted.

Action Step:
Think of the people you want to reach with your show. Think about what topics/words they may use when searching in a podcast app that relates to your show. Now make a list of these keywords. Then play around with possible show titles that include at least one or two of those keywords. Once you've settled on your title, go celebrate! You've reached a HUGE milestone!— woohoo!

"BELIEVE YOU CAN, AND YOU ARE HALFWAY THERE."

- THEODORE ROOSEVELT

SECTION III

BRINGING YOUR IDEA TO LIFE

PODCASTING EQUIPMENT

At the most basic level, the only tools you need in order to start podcasting are a computer and a microphone. So if you're on a tight budget, don't panic! Many a brilliant podcasts were made with just these two pieces of equipment. Assuming you already own a laptop or desktop computer, you will only need to purchase the following equipment in order to make your show:

MICROPHONES

Purchase a USB microphone. This is the type of mic that can plug right into your computer. Make sure it includes "cardioid" pattern recording as a feature (this refers to the shape in which the field of sound is inputed).

The ATR2100 - This is the microphone I used when I started podcasting. It runs for about $99 today.

The Blue Yeti - This is the microphone I currently use. It's a slight step up from the ATR2100. It cost about $130 today.

Please do not use the microphone built into your laptop or phone for recording! If absolutely necessary, you can use a pair of earbuds with a built in mic for your experimental drafts, but your sound quality will be severely reduced, and Pineapple Podcasters don't mess around with sub-par sound quality!

*NOTE - If you are going to be doing field recordings (interviewing in the real world vs. in a studio), you will need a different type of microphone to fit your needs. Look for a good quality "dynamic vocal" mic. There are a lot of factors that go into field recording such as indoor vs. outdoor, power sources, file storage and transfer, portability, number of subjects you are recording, etc. The Shure SM58-LC is a good option for many scenarios, but feel free to explore other options.

ACCESSORIES

Pop Screen - A pop screen or wind screen helps minimize the harsh "P-pop" sounds in your recordings. Your mic will likely have an accessory option for this and I highly recommend you get one. They are usually very cheap ($5-$15).

A Mic Boom - This is a type of stand that gets your mic off your desk in order to minimize vibrations that may transfer to your mic when you write on or touch your desk. If you can afford it, they are nice to have. They range from $30-$200.

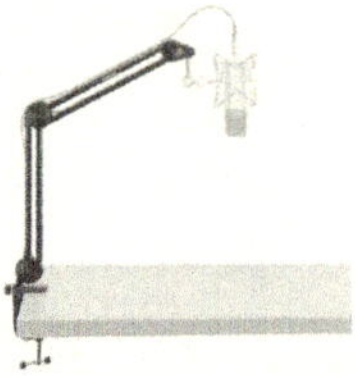

RECORDING SPACE

Where you record your podcast is of the utmost importance. You need to record in a quiet space that preferably has little to no echo. Some podcasters are lucky enough to have a room in their home they can transform into a studio. Others have to get more creative. Higher-budget projects may rent a professional studio space to do their recording.

When recording at home, try to find a space that has few windows (to keep down outside noises), is away from pets and children, and has little echo (such as a large, empty room with lots of hard surfaces).

In a pinch, a clothes closet can make for an excellent podcast studio.

SOUND PANELS

Sound panels can improve your indoor sound quality greatly. They help to capture sound waves and prevent them from bouncing around the room and into your mic.

My first podcast studio was located in my basement, which had a foam floor and very thick stone walls. The sound quality was naturally very good and I did not feel the need to invest in paneling. However, when we moved into a new home, my new studio reflected a lot of sound, resulting in a very echoey recording. To remedy this, I purchased long velvety curtains to cover the large windows, plush rugs for the floors, and home-made sound panels to cover up much of the drywall (more on DIY sound panels below).

Note that sound panels will only help improve the sound quality inside your recording studio, they will not prevent outside noise from coming into your environment. If you live in a noisy place such as a city or loud apartment building, you might need to take extra steps to sound-proof your space. There are many products on the market that can help with this, including foam sprays and tape for windows and doors, and special insulation.

If aesthetics are of no concern, and sound paneling is necessary to get the quality you desire, then I recommend you purchase rolls of cheap sound paneling foam (shaped like egg cartons) to apply to your walls, and possibly the ceiling, which cost on average between $2 - $3 per sq. ft. But if you're looking for a more elevated design for your podcast studio, then you can create beautiful home-made sound panels yourself for around $20-$50 per panel.

MAKING HOMEMADE SOUND PANELS

Cloth shower curtains! You can find some truly beautiful shower curtain designs these days to fit any aesthetic you are going for. They are very large, and relatively cheap ($14-$40). This will be the front of your sound panel.

Next, build a frame out of wood in the exact dimensions you desire for your walls. You can build one giant frame, or cut up your shower curtain into multiple smaller frames to hang. After your frames are built, stretch your shower curtain over the frame and staple tightly in place. Then fill the backside with insulation and hang. There are plenty of great tutorials on Youtube for making homemade sound panels. Just search "Making Your Own DIY Sound Panels."

SOUND EDITING SOFTWARE

Editing is where your podcast comes to life. It's how you

take your show from amateur to professional. The editing process allows you to add in music & sound effects, cut out mistakes, splice together sound bites, and improve the overall quality of your sound. Editing may seem scary at first, but Pineapple Podcasters never let fear get in the way of their success. We'll go over lots of tips and tricks to get you comfortable with the basics of podcast editing.

A laptop or desktop computer will often come with sound editing software installed. If not, you can purchase or download the software yourself. For a Mac you will either need to download GarageBand (free), Audacity (free) or Adobe Audition ($20). For a PC you will need to download Audacity (free) or Adobe Audition ($20).

Personally, I use a Mac computer and have always used GarageBand for my podcast editing; however, as we will discuss in future chapters, I outsource my final sound editing to a professional who does more advanced techniques for me. If you plan to do 100% of your own sound editing, then you will want to use Audacity or Adobe Audition as they allow for the most advanced editing techniques.

Action Step:
Gather your equipment:

- ▷ Microphone to fit your show (studio and/or field recording)
- ▷ Optional: Popscreen and micboom
- ▷ Computer
- ▷ Editing software

READY, SET, RECORD!

Now that you are set up with a computer, a microphone, a place to record, and sound editing software, you can start recording!

If you're feeling ready to record episodes now, here are the steps to begin. If you need to spend more time brainstorming content or structuring a script for yourself, then pay close attention to the next few chapters and come back here when you feel more prepared.

Step 1: Prepare for action! Have your notes, script, or layout in front of you to help you stay focused and organized.

Step 2: Plug in your mic and open up your sound editing software.

Step 3: Create a new file. If prompted to choose between types of inputs, select the most logical option, such as "mic" or "voice."

Step 4: Adjust your microphone input volume and settings. Input is the level of volume at which your voice will be recorded. If your input level is too low you'll sound too quiet and far away. If your input level is too high, you'll sound blown out and harsh. Watch the video below on how to adjust your input volume and find the correct level. Scan the QR code below with your smartphone camera, or go to vimeo.com/433474951 to watch the tutorial video.

Step 5: Hit record! If you mess up, don't worry, you'll edit that out later. Just keep on recording.

Step 6: After recording, playback some of your track to make sure it recorded properly. Then name and save your file in a way that's easy for you to find.

Pro Tip: Hidden Echo and Reverb

Since many sound-editing softwares, such as GarageBand, are designed for musicians and not podcasters, they may have preset reverb and echo settings installed. This can result in unwanted effects in your recordings. This video by Toby Ryan shows how to turn these pre-installed settings off in GarageBand: youtu.be/mZob1lPNuB4

RECORDING INTERVIEWS

If you have an interview-based podcast, you will need to take a few extra steps to be able to record both yourself and your interviewee's voice.

If you are recording in the same room with your interviewee, make sure you and your interviewee are well mic'd. You may be able to use one microphone for everyone, but for best sound quality, use one mic per person.

If your interviewee is long distance, they will need a USB mic on their end as well. I used to allow my guests to use earbuds or built-in mics, and I'm here to tell you, don't make that same mistake. To ensure good quality from your guests, your options include either purchasing an extra mic yourself and mailing it to them (make sure to include a return label and safe packaging) or insist your guests acquire a USB mic themselves — I recommend the K669B Fifine USB mic, which runs about $40. I once had a guests cancel on me because she didn't want to spend the money on a decent microphone, only to write me back weeks later saying she'd still love to come onto my show and she now had the proper equipment. Stick to your guns when it comes to sound quality.

Most podcasters, myself included, record interviews online using a special app or program. Personally I have yet to find an affordable option for capturing good quality recordings via phone. Avoid this route or do extensive research on your best options if you're insistent on trying. Also, apps like FaceTime, Google Hangout, or Messenger Video, are not reliable, as they are not designed for capturing quality two-track recordings. There are many different options for recording interviews online. Here's a few that have worked well for me:

Skype - Skype is my favorite choice for recording interviews. I have found the sound quality to be better than Zoom (another popular choice), plus it's free. You will, however, need to purchase a program called Ecamm Recorder to be able to record interviews on Skype (approx. $40, one-time fee). If your interviewee doesn't already have a Skype account they'll have to create one (for free) and then connect with you before the interview. Skype will sometimes have bad days where things just act glitchy. This happens with most internet-based programs.

Zoom - Zoom is a popular choice for interviewing people via the internet. It's approximately $15 per month to use for more than 40 minutes at a time. The advantage is that your interviewee only needs to click on a link to join your call (versus Skype where they have to create an account and find you). The disadvantage is that the sound quality is slightly lower than Skype.

Zencastr - Zencastr is very popular in the podcasting world. It is an online platform similar to Zoom, but designed for better sound quality. Advantages are that it's user friendly for you and your interviewee (you just have to give your guest a link to click on and it will automatically join them into the call), and the sound quality is high. The downside is that it's pricier ($20/mo if you record more than 8 hrs/mo. Less than that is free). I have heard many people give positive feedback for Zencastr, but personally, I did not have a good experience. I found that the two tracks (my voice and my interviewee's voice) would get out of sync in the recording, resulting in me having to edit a lot more in post production. This seemed to be a common issue according to the Zencastr technical support for certain users/browsers. Eventually I gave up and went back to using Skype.

Separate Local Recordings - This method involves you recording directly into your computer and instructing your interviewee to do the same on their end. If your interviewee is a Mac users, the easiest route is to have them use Quicktime Player. If they are a PC user, they may not have a preinstalled recording app and you will be unable to use this method. I like to count to three and both press record at the same time so it's easier to match up the files in editing. After recording, your interviewee sends you their file (I use WeTransfer.com for this) and you match the two tracks up in your editing software. The advantage of this method is that, when done right, you will get a great sound quality result. The disadvantage is that you are relying on your interviewee not to mess anything up on their end! I once had to redo an entire interview because my guest thought they had hit record on their end but actually hadn't.

TWO TRACK RECORDING

As you will see in the chapters regarding editing, podcast life becomes MUCH easier when interviews are recorded on two separate tracks. This means that, if you, the host, start coughing or sneezing in the middle of a brilliant sound bite from your guest, that's ok. You can just cut out the sound of you coughing on your own track and no one will even know. This also ensures that you can match the volume levels in case one person's mic has a higher input volume than the other.

ENABLING TWO TRACK RECORDING ON SKYPE

- Make sure you have downloaded the Skype app for your

computer and created an account for free. The app will live in your applications folder. Don't use Skype through your browser.

- Make sure you have purchased and installed Ecamm Recorder for Skype (the software required to record Skype interviews). When you open Skype, the Ecamm Recorder will appear in a separate window labeled "Call Recorder." It looks like this:

- In the small "Call Recorder" box, click on the settings icon.

- Once in "Settings," click on "Recording Options," and select "Multi-Track."

For best quality, change your setting to look like this:

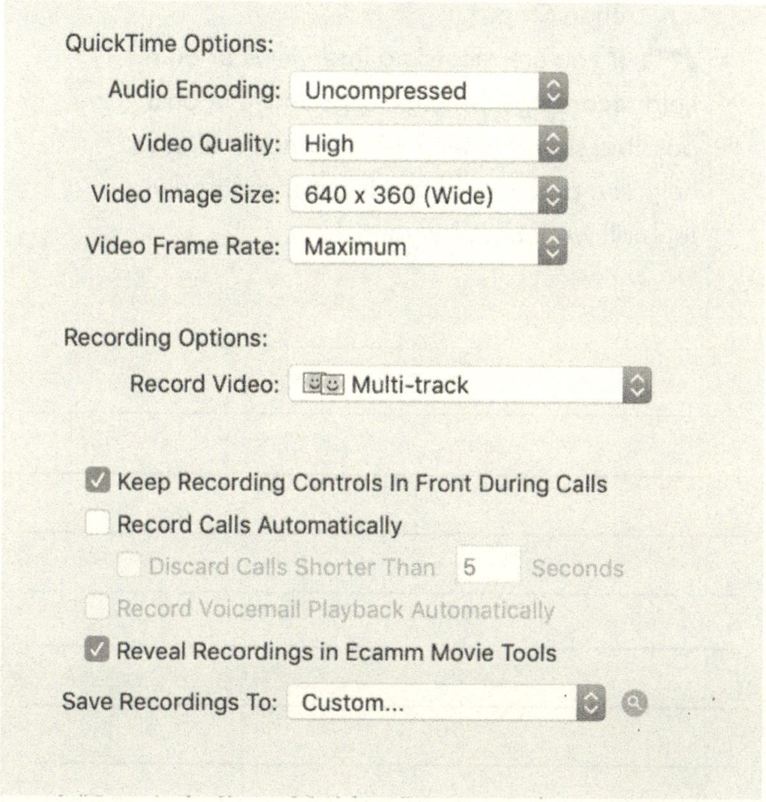

ENABLING TWO TRACK RECORDING ON ZOOM

- Open Zoom and select "Preferences."
- Select "Recording."
- Check the box that says "Record a separate audio file for each participant."
- Test this method out, as Zoom is known to change their setting functions periodically.

Action Step:
If you are recording interviews or doing field recordings, practice capturing the best possible sound quality. Find friends willing to help you practice using whatever method you feel will work best for your show.

TIPS FOR CONDUCTING GREAT INTERVIEWS

Great content and good conversations are what your audience are here for, so let's make sure they get it.

Interviewing skills don't develop overnight. They get honed with time and practice. Oftentimes, a new podcast host will just hit record and ramble, assuming that their charismatic personality alone will create the content they're looking for. Pineapple Podcasters don't make this mistake. Even if you're new, you can keep these tips on interviewing in mind right from the start:

- Bring the energy! Your audience may not see your face, but they can certainly detect lethargy in your voice. People are typically drawn to happy, energetic, and lively people, so do whatever it takes to get your energy up — jumping jacks, panting like a dog, or a good old fashion Cup O' Joe can help ensure a lively recording.

- Have a goal for each interview/episode. What specifically are you wanting your audience to glean from your guest? Use this as a roadmap for your entire interview to help keeps things relevant.

- Create an experience. Hosting a show is like hosting a

party, you want everyone (your guest, your audience, and yourself) to have a great time. Throughout your interview, ask yourself if the moments you're creating are exciting enough for people to talk about when it's over. Create "shareable moments!"

- Don't ask unnecessary questions. If you find yourself asking a question just to fill space, it's better to just pause, take a moment to collect your thoughts, and edit out the awkward silence later.

- Prepare yourself AND your guest. Before each interview, I provide questions to my guest so that they can really crush it. It's important, however, to actively listen and not hold onto your pre-arranged questions too tightly so that you don't miss out on organic moments or key follow-up questions. I once interviewed an Olympic gold medalist about his use of essential oils for performance, but once I learned that he was passionate about supporting sports programs for troubled youth, I shifted the conversation as to not deprive my audience of such inspiring content.

- Set expectations. Tell your guest exactly what you're looking for. The more specific you are about WHY your audience is tuning in, the more your guests can provide relevant content. Also, make all technical requirements loud and clear. I repeatedly tell my guests that all interviews take place on Skype and that a USB mic is required. If they aren't prepared with either of those things we do not record.

- Study up! Intentionally listen to great interviews like Oprah Winfrey, Ira Glass, Barber Walters, Marie Forleo, and Phoebe Judge (*Criminal* podcast), and apply what you notice. Through active study of other interviewers, I've improved greatly in my own skills over the years. I've learned how to change the subject more organically, interject my own thoughts without being rude, when to lean into a question further, and different ways to respond to statements besides continually saying "Uh-huh," "I see," and "Yeah, that's cool."

- As the host, you act as a conduit between your audience and your guest, so channel their curiosity into your conversations. Ask the hard questions in the back of your listener's mind. What would they ask if they were in the room? Don't be shy about sharing your own opinions from time to time either. Your audience wants to hear from you— your reactions, your thoughts, your insights. Be the captain of your audience's experience and steer each new interview with confidence.

- One last tip to make your editing process go ten times faster: Have your notes in front of you during your interview. Jot down the time stamp of any place you want to go back and fix. If a dog starts to bark, or you completely fumble a question, write down the time and fix it during post-production.

Action Step:

Get in the mindset of a great interviewer:

▷ Listen to an entire episode of your favorite interview-based podcast and take notes about what you like and dislike about the way the interviewer conducts themself.

▷ The next time you are at a party, try talking one-on-one with people and asking them thoughtful questions about their life. As a bonus, you'll make lots of new friends (people love talking about themselves). Take this challenge up a notch by avoiding the word "I." This is very challenging, but will teach you how to keep the conversation focused on others, which is an important part of being a great interviewer.

PODCAST EDITING

Once you've recorded some sound bites, a few interviews, or some great content, what happens next?

This is where the magic happens! The editing process is going to look different for each podcaster. Your show may require very little editing (such as a show with one host who can spout off great content that needs little reworking). Or maybe your show consists of lots of different sound bites and sound effects all coming together perfectly in post-production, in which case, you could spend hours editing just one episode.

Whatever software you use, you may need to watch some tutorial videos to learn how to do basic sound editing. Don't worry, you will be able to handle most, if not all, of your show's editing needs.

In the following video, I'll show you what editing looks like for my podcast in Garageband. You'll see first-hand how to:

- Start a new project and deactivate that pesky metronome.
- Split a sound file into two separate tracks.
- Import sound files into GarageBand.

- Make cuts and rearrange sound bites.
- Splice sounds together smoothly.
- Insert intros, outros, and music.
- Export files in the correct format.

For a basic tutorial of what editing looks like for my show, scan the QR code or go to youtu.be/vedXA0hYXsw

ADVANCED EDITING OPTIONS

As you saw in the video above, I choose to outsource the advanced editing for my show (like adding in music, sound effects, and equalizing volume levels). This costs me, on average, $115 per month ($25-$35 per episode). To me, this $115 is well worth it as it saves me many long hours in the editing room doing things I am not trained to do. I highly recommend outsourcing if you plan to monetize your podcast.

If you choose to do your own advanced editing, more power to you! This will give you lots of freedom to experiment as well as save you money. You can find many advanced training videos for sound editing on YouTube or in your sound editing software's help section. You can also use a service such as Auphonic to polish up your sound.

Auphonic is a web-based service that takes care of many advanced sound editing techniques. It is user friendly and very affordable. It is free to use for up to 2 hours of sound editing per month, then goes up to $11 per month or more depending on how much sound you'll be polishing.

Auphonic will:

- Balance levels between speakers, music and speech — no compressor knowledge required.
- Normalize loudness between speakers and entire tracks.
- Automatically reduce noise and hum, and filter disturbing low frequencies.

TIPS FOR OUTSOURCING YOUR EDITING

If you choose to work with a professional sound editor you will need to vet them properly. Websites such as Upwork or Fiverr make it easy to connect with freelance professionals. This is how I found my podcast editor who I still use to this day. These platforms are free to use but take a fee each time you pay your contractor. The cost of services is negotiable between you and your freelancer. In the beginning, I paid roughly $25 per episode to my sound editor.

To find an editor for your show, put out an ad on Upwork or Fiverr, or search through candidates on these platforms who specialize in "podcast sound editing."

When I was looking to hire, I took one of my very first interviews and sent it to candidates asking them to send back a sample of how they could improve the sound quality. I ended up choosing my editor because he was one of the few candidates who responded quickly and took the time to not only polish up the sample I gave, but also offered amazing advice on how to improve my sound quality during the recording process. He was genuinely excited about my show topic and even gave me some tips on how to grow my podcast.

Whoever you choose, make sure that they communicate well, are timely in their editing (a 2-3 day turnaround is a reasonable expectation), and they charge a sustainable rate. My editor lives in Serbia, and charges $25 to edit a 30 minute or less episode. This rate may vary depending on the country your editor lives in and their experience level.

Upwork and Fiverr make it easy to pay your freelancer through their platforms. If you hire someone independently then they should send you timely invoices. If they are in the U.S. you will need to collect a W9 form and send them a 1099 tax form at the end of each year.

Your editor will instruct you on how to send them your files and other information they require.

TAGGING YOUR FILES

Ever notice when you listen to a podcast or music that certain information gets displayed on your device — like the song title, artist name, album, or genre? Ever wonder how album artwork gets paired with the right song tracks? It all happens thanks to tagging! Tagging allows you to attach certain information, such as your episode title and cover art, to your final sound file so that it gets displayed properly on your listener's device.

Tagging can be done by yourself or your editor. It's a necessary step for a professional looking podcast, so don't skip it — but I don't have to tell you that — you're a Pineapple Podcaster, you're not cutting corners!

For a short tutorial on how to tag your files, scan the QR code or go to youtu.be/qDTvVYNSKsg:

LAST BUT NOT LEAST

After recording and editing a few tracks, an amateur would jump straight to launching their podcast, but for a Pineapple Podcaster, things are just about to get juicy! With a little patience, experimentation, and elbow grease, you can apply some finishing touches that can make the difference between a 'never-heard-of-it' podcast, and an 'OMG-did-you-hear-that-episode' podcast.

Unless you've already announced it to the world, no one is sitting around yelling at you because you haven't launched your podcast yet — so take your time to experiment before settling into your final sound.

Get creative, try new things, play around with aspects of the editing, sound effects, content, format, length, etc. If you struggle with procrastination, set yourself a due date for wrapping up the experiments. Write down when you will be hitting the publish button. Don't let perfectionism get in the way of launching. An imperfect podcast will always trump a perfect one that never launched.

INTROS, OUTROS, AND JINGLES

What would *Golden Girls* be without the iconic "Thank you for being a friend?" Or imagine *Wheel of Fortune* without the telltale chant of "WHEEL OF FORTUNE!"

Intros and jingles are NOT mandatory for your podcast, but they can be an easy and fun way to establish your show's brand.

Every podcast has its own unique way of starting off their episodes. As you'll soon learn, consistency is King, so once you pick a style, stick with it! Here's some examples of formats that are popular:

- **A Jingle** - A short theme song - oftentimes light and funny, such as the *Bad With Money* podcast, or the *Story Pirates* podcast.

- **Sound Bite** - An intriguing sound clip taken from what's to come in the episode, such as the *Sword and Scale* podcast.

- **Intro with Music** - Theme-fitting background music with explanative narration such as *The No Sleep Podcast.*

When it comes to your show's intro, there are no hard and fast rules. You may want to jump straight to the content, or drop your theme-music in after a long teaser. You may choose to have music with words, music without words, a loud sound effect, or your standalone voice. For inspiration and ideas, listen to the intros, music, and formats of some of my favorite podcasts:

- Radiolab
- Reply All
- More Perfect
- Up And Vanished

- Bad with Money
- Serial (Season 1)

Compare these intros to how the infamous *This American Life* creates their indistinguishable branding. The show has no set theme or music. Instead, Ira Glass begins each episode with a thought or idea that leads the listener into the story. His unmistakable voice, combined with his eclectic music selection are what make the show so recognizable. Bottom line: you don't always need a jingle, sound effect, or intro to create your show branding.

TIP - Keep your intro short and sweet! If you decide to create a jingle or theme music, make sure it's short enough that people won't be tempted to skip through it after a few episodes. 20 seconds maximum is best.

If you choose to create a jingle or standard intro, you can make it yourself or hire a professional musician or voice-over artist. I was surprised how affordable it was to hire a voice-over actor through Fiverr. After layering the voiceover on top of some snazzy background music I fell in love! I've used the same recording as my show's intro since day one.

A great place to find royalty free background music is AudioJungle.net, or your can work with a sound artist through Upwork.com or hire a musician friend to create something unique for your show.

Whatever you choose, stay kosher. Make sure you have full royalty rights to any music you use. Don't steal music!

COVER ART

Before you can publish your show, you will need to create some cover art for it. This cover art is displayed in every podcast app and website that your show is published on.

While some novice podcasters may skimp or short-cut this step, a Pineapple Podcaster ensures that their cover art helps them stand out.

Take your time and design something you truly love. Your podcast cover art will be displayed anywhere your podcast is available to listen, including iTunes, Spotify, Stitcher, etc. You can update and change your cover art as often as you like.

Good podcast cover art should be simple in design, have bold colors and contrast, and contain minimal text that is large enough to read on a small screen. When reviewing your cover art ideas, make sure you take a moment to view the design on a small screen. Does it hold up when shrunk?

Parameters for creating podcast cover art are as follows:

- File must be a JPEG or PNG file.
- File must be in RGB color format (most automatically are, so don't worry if you don't know what this means).
- File must be a minimum size of 1400 x 1400 pixels and a maximum size of 3000 x 3000 pixels.

You can create your own podcast cover art using a program like Canva (a free design program that's easy for beginners), or outsource this task to a designer.

Options for outsourcing your cover art include:

- Fiverr.com.
- 99designs.
- Hire a graphic artist from a local design company or from Upwork.com.

Notice how the following podcast covers are easy to read, are visually appealing, and give a sense of what the show is about before even listening to it:

Action Step:

- ▷ Make a list of ideas for your jingle or intro, and cover art.
- ▷ Set your budget and timeframe for these items and make an action plan that keeps you within that range.
- ▷ If your budget doesn't allow for hiring artists, get creative! Make a list of friends you may be able to barter or trade with for their services.

"HAVE ENOUGH
COURAGE TO START
AND ENOUGH HEART
TO FINISH."

- JESSICA N.S. YOURKO

SECTION IV
LAUNCHING

CONSISTENCY IS KING

Imagine you turn on your TV and go to the weather channel, only to find that today, they're airing cartoons instead. Or, imagine sitting down to watch an episode of Jeopardy, but today Alex Trebek has decided to sing show tunes for 30 minutes. You would be confused as all get-out! Viewers like to know what to expect when tuning into a certain program. They thrive on predictability and consistency.

If you're watching a house remodeling show, the format will usually go something like this: find ugly house, fix it up, show the beautiful finished project, couple is happy. If today's episode starts off with a crime-scene and a house that won't be remodeled till they discover who committed the murder, the formula would be broken, you'd probably stop watching, and the director would likely be fired.

Pineapple Podcasters treat their podcast like a television production. They keep their show consistent, so that viewers know what to expect when they tune in. They don't make a 10 minute episode one day and then a 30 minute one the next. They have certain routines that they do for each show, such as start each episode off with a jingle, or ending with a 2-minute guided meditation. They keep these routines consistent for their listeners. They don't promise an episode once a week then flake out for months. They don't release new episodes daily than all of a sudden change to once a week without warning.

For example, listen to a few episodes of *Circle Round*, an amazing podcast for kids and adults that shares adapted folktales from around the world. Every time I tune into Circle Round (usually while driving my kids to school), I know my experience will include the following rituals; First, I will learn the country that the folktale originates from. Second, I will hear unique and classical instruments highlighting the story. Third, I will hear professional actors reading the lines of the characters. Fourth, I will be prompted with a learning lesson at the end of the story, such as; "Kids, ask your parents about a time that they made a mistake, and how they fixed it." These elements, repeated during each episode, help the listener know what to expect and look forward to each time.

MEDIA HOST

In order to put your podcast out into the world, you'll want to utilize what's called a media host. A media host is essentially a home for you podcast. It gives you a streamlined way to organize details, track statistics, and publish album artwork. But MOST importantly, a media host provides you with your show's RSS feed (or Really Simple Syndication). An RSS feed looks like this: www.yourshowname.com/rss. With this RSS feed, you can now submit your show to platforms such as iTunes and Spotify, and hence the world.

You only have to submit your RSS feed one time to these platforms. After that, every change you make gets automatically communicated between your media host and the platforms you've been published on.

Here's what the process of setting up a media host and publishing it to iTunes looks like:

- Step 1: Choose your media host (we'll compare options later).

- Step 2: Set up your show details in your media host: title, album artwork, author name, podcast category, description, and so on.

- Step 3: Upload episodes. Don't worry, they won't be available to the public till you select a publish date or hit "publish now."

- Step 4: Copy down your RSS feed (it's usually located in the "destinations" section of your media host).

- Step 5: Go to the iTunes publishing website (itunesconnect.apple.com) and submit your RSS feed. I go over these steps in detail in the tutorial video at the end of this chapter.

- Step 6: Wait for word from iTunes that you've been published. Now every episode you publish or update on your media host will show up live in iTunes for all to see.

CHOOSING A MEDIA HOST

There are many options when it comes to choosing a media host. Here are a few you can explore:

- **Libsyn**: Libsyn is what I use for all my podcast hosting, and I am a proud affiliate for their services. They are affordable, reputable, provide detailed statistics, and have been around since the beginning of podcasting. If you plan on monetizing your podcast, having the kind of detailed statistics Libsyn provides is a must. If this is the route you choose, you can use coupon code "SAM," when creating your account. This will get you approximately two months of free service. To get the most out of your free trial, start your account on the 2nd day of the month. This will give you the remainder of that month plus the next full month for free. Libsyn cost

$5-$75 per month based on the amount of content you are uploading.

- **Podbean**: Podbean is a great choice for beginner podcasters on a tight budget. Podbean is free so long as you stay under a certain amount of uploads per month. Podbean also provides you with a very basic website for your podcast. The downsides are that they provide limited statistics and customization of your site. If you expect to monetize and grow your audience quickly, the lack of statistics will prove challenging, but if you are just starting out or looking to experiment, Podbean is a great option.

- **Buzzsprout**: If you're looking for the easiest, quickest, and most user-friendly option for getting your podcast launched quickly, then Buzzsprout was designed for you. However, they are more expensive than most other options and are not capable of complex podcast tasks such as interfacing with your website, or obtaining detailed statistics.

Other options (some of which are free) include the following. Keep in mind that free services will not likely provide statistics, which is very important when you move towards monetizing your podcast:

- Anchor
- Blubrry
- Spreaker

- Podiant

Don't labor forever over choosing a media host — you can always change it later (though it's a bit of a process). Look at current blog articles and tutorial videos of each platform to find the media host that fits you best

HITTING PUBLISH AND SUBMITTING TO PLATFORMS

Once you've chosen your media host, you can upload your content, set up your show details, and submit your show to iTunes and other platforms.

Hold your horses on that publish button though until you've finished the chapters on "Monetizing."

Scan the QR code or go to vimeo.com/366556601 for a step-by-step tutorial of what that process looks like for Libsyn users.

Action Step:
Research different media hosts and decide what will work best to suit your goals. Then watch the tutorial video above to learn how to set up your show details and submit to iTunes and other destinations.

LAUNCH STRATEGIES

Podcasters always wonder how often they should release episodes. The answer is, it's entirely up to you! Some podcasts produce a new episode every single day. Others create new episodes once a month. Some shows create content seasonally, releasing a series of episodes all at once a few times a year. There are very successful podcasts on all ends of this spectrum.

The frequency of your podcast will depend largely on how long it takes to create your content. Some content, such as investigative reporting, in-depth explorations, or complicated undertakings take weeks, or even months to produce just one episode. Some content, such as a single-host show, or simple interview formats are a little bit faster to produce and can drop more frequently.

The only two questions you must ask yourself before committing to a production schedule are these:

- What will your audience like?
- And what can you realistically manage to produce?

Once you begin publishing your content, stay consistent with it. This will go miles in helping your fans stay engaged and interested. I recommend you have at least a months worth of content ready to go before hitting the publish button. This will allow you plenty of buffer time as you navigate your content rhythm.

YOUR FIRST FEW EPISODES

When podcasting was newer, many hosts would launch their shows with an "episode 0." Episode 0 was usually less than 5 minutes long and acted as a sort of introduction to the show. The host would explain what the show was about and introduce themselves to the listeners. In my opinion, today's audiences no longer need or want an "episode 0." They want to see for themselves what your show has to offer them. Only when they like it will they care to learn about who you are and why you started your podcast. I'm not trying to be harsh, but honestly, if you're starting from zero, you have to earn the trust of your listeners by providing good quality content before you have the right to blab on about yourself and why you created your podcast.

I recommend you make your first few episodes as power-punched as possible — full of content that showcases your podcast's unique qualities and serves your audience well. Slip in some details about yourself and why you started your podcast, but do so sparingly and only after you've served some great content.

A newer trend I'm seeing (and loving), are podcast trailers. These have essentially replaced the outdated "episode 0" with short, intriguing, and well polished teasers akin to a powerful movie trailer. Think marketing! A podcast trailer sitting on your show's published iTunes page is not only shareable, but allows listeners to hit that "Subscribe" button and be alerted for when your first episode drops.

When planning out your first few episodes, keep the following tips in mind:

- Use keywords in your episode titles that will help your target audience find your show faster.

- Craft your first episodes to really shine. Go the extra mile to cut down the fluff and get to the point. Spend some time polishing your sound effects (if you use any) and getting a great sound quality.

- Don't be a perfectionist. This may seem contrary to the above tips, but getting your show launched today versus 6 months from today is way more important than getting it perfect. If you need to ignore some of my advice about cutting down fluff, maximizing keywords, or prioritizing sound quality for the sake of just getting it done, then by all means do so. Capitalize on the momentum and excitement that comes with a new project by setting a launch date that takes precedence over perfection.

- If you have an interview-based show, try your best to launch with some power-packed special guests. Reach out to the mini-celebrities within your niche and invite them on as a guest of your soon-to-launch podcast. They may just say yes, and this will give your show a huge boost in authority from the start. The worst that can happen is that they say no or never reply to your request.

Action Step:
Make a dream list of top guests and/or top content and keywords you may want to showcase in your early episodes. Craft your early episodes accordingly.

RATINGS AND REVIEWS

Launching the first few episodes is one of the most exciting moments in a podcaster's journey! But what happens next? How will people find you? How will you grow? How will you monetize?

When it comes to creating a successful podcast long-term, you'll want to do everything you can to maximize your launch early on.

iTunes and other podcast apps have algorithms that determine which shows show up in search results or in category pages. These algorithms are affected by your download numbers, your show title, and episode titles (keywords), and by the number of ratings and reviews your show has received. Rating and review numbers are weighed very heavily in these algorithms. Getting more ratings and reviews will help your podcast be exponentially more findable, as well as give it a sense of prestige and authority.

Ask and you shall receive.

In your first few episodes, be sure to ask your listeners to leave you a rating and review. Explain how to do that (it's not very intuitive for most people). Text friends and family and ask them to leave you a review to help you out.

Consider incentivizing ratings and reviews as well. Perhaps you can do a giveaway for those who leave you a rating and review during your first month of launching. This is a little bit tricky to accomplish since iTunes and other podcast destinations do not share user data directly with you, but it can be well worth your time to troubleshoot. To do a giveaway you'll have to instruct your listeners to leave you a review then go to your website and enter their name into a giveaway form (I use Google Forms for this).

I launched my podcast with a giveaway in exchange for reviews during the first few weeks of my show's launch and it resulted in getting hundreds of reviews. This in turn helped give my show more prestige as well as made it rank higher in the iTunes algorithm (it made my show more findable!).

Action Step:
List 10 friends and family members that you're gong to ask to rate and review your show upon launch. If planning a giveaway or incentive, list ideas and estimate the cost — don't forget shipping!

OTHER PEOPLE'S PLATFORMS

By now you should have a good understanding of who your ideal listeners are; the people you are trying to serve and add value to with your podcast.

Think about where your ideal listeners are already hanging out online and use what the amazing Marie Forleo calls "Other People's Platforms" to tell them about your show.

For example, when I launched *The Essential Oil Revolution*, I knew that I wanted to serve people who were hungry for all things essential-oil related. I knew of many Facebook groups with thousands of active members that focused on essential oils, so I spent a LOT of time in these groups leading up to my podcast launch. I was active in the conversations, regularly posting, and building authentic relationships with the key leaders and members in those groups. So, when it came time to launch my show it was very easy for me to ask an admin for permission to share my new podcast with the community. Oftentimes they would share it themselves because they knew their community would get value from my show. This helped me establish my initial listener base quickly from the start.

Keep in mind that in order to use "Other People's Platforms," you must first and foremost ask permission from the owner of that platform. Don't just join a Facebook group and start spamming about your new podcast. That's just gross. Earn your right to share by first giving back. Be interactive, be helpful, and be nice!

Think long and hard about your target audience and where they spend their time online. Are any of these places a good fit for you to get the news out about your podcast?

Here are some prompts to help you dig deeper into this strategy. Ask yourself:

- What blogs do my ideal listeners read? Could I offer to write a guest post for this blog?
- What Facebook groups do my ideal listeners hang out in? How can I build relationships and add value to these communities?
- Are there any active online chatrooms/community spaces about my topic? How can I interact positively there?
- What other podcasts would my ideal listeners already be tuning into? Can I be a guest on those shows or ask those hosts to promote my show via a paid ad or trade?
- What events do my ideal listeners attend? Is it possible to sponsor this event or have a booth there?
- What other opportunities might there be to meet and reach my ideal listeners?

LAUNCHING WITH A BANG

You've created your first few episodes, you've set up your media host, you've uploaded your beautiful cover art, you've submitted your show to iTunes and other podcast destinations, and you've set your first episodes to go live soon. Congratulations! You are now officially a podcaster!!!

Now it's time to tell the world about it. Just like the grand opening of a new restaurant or store, there is a lot of excitement surrounding something new. Use this to your advantage and tell everyone you can about it. Don't keep it to yourself and hope that people will somehow magically find you. Share it on social media, share it to your friends, your family, your kid's teachers, your fitness trainer, your monthly book club, your church…everyone!

Celebrate your victories along the way. Did you reach 500 downloads? Did you reach 5,000 downloads? Shout it from the rooftops! Then go throw yourself a party. You deserve it!

"SUCCESS IS NOT
THE RESULT OF
MAKING MONEY;
EARNING MONEY IS THE
RESULT OF SUCCESS"

- EARL NIGHTINGALE

SECTION V
MONETIZING

HOW TO MAKE MONEY IN PODCASTING

Monetizing is something I love helping new podcasters do right from the start. Even if your audience is small, there are plenty of ways for you to earn money.

There's one very important rule that a true Pineapple Podcaster will follow when it comes to monetization: ALWAYS ALWAYS ALWAYS serve your audience first!

Never sell or advertise a product/service that doesn't serve them well. Never put your name behind something you don't believe in. And always keep your listeners' interests at the forefront of your mind.

Also, don't get caught up in "analysis paralysis." You may not have the perfect plan in place for monetization right now, and that's ok. For now, just focus on building trust with your audience by serving them amazing content that they love. Be authentic. Be real. Be passionate. Be consistent. Show up for your people and they will show up for you down the road. You cannot sell to someone who doesn't trust you. So while the below strategies for monetizing are tried and true, none of them will work if you don't first and foremost serve your audience.

Now let's explore some of the common methods for monetizing a podcast:

Digital Products - Create a digital product such as an ebook or online course that you know your audience would love, and tell them about it on your show. For example, I monetize my show by offering my *Classroom in a Box* digital files for people wanting to teach essential oil classes in their community. It's full of scripts, handouts, and tips for holding a successful essential oils class.

Provide a Service - Are you a health coach? A life coach? An amazing accountant? Podcasting is a fantastic way to get more clients. Tell your audience how to sign up for a consultation. *The Life Coach School* podcast is a great example of this. Listen to the last 60 seconds or so of practically any episode to see how she monetizes her products effectively and tastefully. Keep in mind who you are attracting with your content and be sure your services are relevant to that target audience. You may be the best chef in the world, but if your show is all about Crop Circles, don't expect your audience to shell out for the new cook book you wrote — they may take you up on your custom tailored tinfoil hats though!

Affiliate Advertising - Many companies will pay you commission if you refer your listeners to their products or services. For example, I am an affiliate for an essential oil accessories company that sells things like oil diffusers, oil travel bags, oil-themed t-shirts, and more. Every now and then I will talk about this company on my show and why I love them, and explain how my listeners can get a discount on their first order by using my coupon code. Every time someone uses my coupon code I earn a commission on that sale.

Think about companies that would be a good fit for your audience and reach out to ask them if you can become an affiliate for them. Most sponsors will send you samples of their products and ask you to talk briefly about your personal experience with them, and will tell you of any mandatory things to say during your ad. If you can't think of a good company to fit your show, then consider signing up to be an affiliate for Amazon and Audible. It's easy and free for anyone to do this. Direct your listeners to a page on your website that lists your affiliate links. It doesn't cost them any extra when they shop and it's an easy way for your listeners to support your show.

Subscriptions/Donations - Some shows offer bonus content or exclusive perks to listeners who donate or support their show via patron donations. Services like Patreon or Libsyn have programs to help podcasters set up apps or subscription sites for this. A good example of this is the *Sleep With Me* Podcast (that show we talked about before that helps you fall asleep fast). Another example is the *In The Dark* podcast. Occasionally, *In The Dark* will create new episodes that are only accessible to donors.

Paid Advertising - Once your podcast reaches a consistent download rate, many companies will pay you to read ads for their products/services on your show. If you're looking for inspiration on creating brilliant and creative ads, I highly recommend you tune into the ad spots on the *Reply All* podcast — they are hilarious, genuine, and holy un-skippable.

PAID ADVERTISING EXPLAINED

If you plan to work with paid sponsors there are some important things to be aware of.

In order to start working with sponsors for paid advertising, you'll want to aim for having a steady 5,000 downloads or more per episode. However, some ad agencies are willing to work with smaller shows in the case of very niche target audiences.

In order to do paid advertising you will need access to your show's stats from your media host, so be sure to choose your media host plan accordingly.

Compared to affiliate advertising where you only get paid a commission if your advertisement results in a sale, the paid advertising model works with what's known as a CPM rate. CPM stands for "Cost Per Mile" and in podcasting this means the cost per 1,000 downloads.

If, for example, a sponsor is willing to pay you a CPM rate of $25 (aka $25 for every 1,000 downloads of an episode) and your show guaranteed at least 5,000 downloads an episode (aka 5 CPM "miles"), then you would receive $125 for an ad read with that sponsor (5 x $25 = $125).

Some advertisers pay different rates depending on the length of the ad (30 secs, 60 secs, 90 secs, etc).

There is still much debate over what a "fair" CPM rate is for podcast advertising. Ultimately this decision is up to the podcaster. I have seen rates as high as $55 CPM and as low as $15 CPM.

BAKED-IN VS. DYNAMIC AD INSERTION

Have you ever binged on a podcast and been forced to skip over the same exact ad read over and over again? If so, then you have experienced what's known as "dynamic ad insertion," a method of podcast advertising that grew in popularity in 2017.

Beginner podcasters, or smaller shows typically stick with "baked-in" advertising. This means when you read an ad, it lives inside that episode's recording permanently.

But with "dynamic ad insertion," ads change on demand for each episode. Dynamic ad technology allows you to designate specific spots in your episode where ads can be inserted, and then you can change *the ad portion* of that episode whenever you want to. In other words, you could swap in a brand new ad into an episode you may have published 3 years ago without having to upload a whole new file to your media host.

For example, let's say an advertiser pays you for 10,000 "impressions" of their ad (an "impression" is defined as each time an episode is downloaded with that particular ad in it). This means they will pay you to run their ad up until 10,000 people have heard it — right now, most technologies cannot tell when a listener skips over an ad, so it's all based on your download rate. In this scenario, you would program your dynamic ad technology to only serve that particular ad up to 10,000 times, then automatically switch that ad spot out for a completely different one, or take it out altogether. This allows for much more long-term income opportunity for your show since you can continually update ad spots when advertisers are willing to pay for impressions.

Dynamic ad insertion requires advanced technology, planning, and know-how. But if your show reaches into the higher download rates (let's say around 15,000 downloads or more per episode), then this highly customizable and efficient form of advertising is well worth considering. For more information on dynamic ad insertion, talk with your media host customer service and request resources specific to their platform.

HOW DO YOU FIND SPONSORS?

To find sponsors for your show you can either go the DIY approach or work with an ad agency.

If you go the DIY route you will be responsible for finding, negotiating, and writing up contracts with advertisers. You know your audience best. If you know of a company that your listeners would adore, try reaching out to that company and see if they'd be interested in sponsoring your show. Hire a lawyer to make up a contract you can use with advertisers, or write one yourself using an online template. Just be aware that business laws vary by country and state.

If negotiating and writing up sponsorship contracts intimidates you, consider linking arms with a podcast sponsorship agency. These businesses can connect you to potential advertisers, negotiate deals and contracts on your behalf, and schedule ad reads for you. The agency simply takes a small cut in return for this service, and in my opinion is well worth it.

When my podcast reached a steady rate of 5,000+ downloads per episode I started working with an ad agency. I loved not having to do all of the work of finding and contracting with sponsors myself. For the past few years I've been working with an agency that specializes in sponsorship for small-scale woman-owned podcasts.Their name is True Native Media and I absolutely love working with them.

Pro-Tip: If you plan to one day go the route of paid advertising, make sure you set your podcast audience up for this precedent from the start. If you run your podcast completely ad free for months and then all of a sudden start including ads, your audience will likely be annoyed. Include ad spots in your show from the beginning by becoming an Amazon or Audible affiliate, pitching your own product, or simply advertising that people should join your newsletter, subscribe to your podcast, or leave you a review. The important thing is to get your listeners used to being "sold" to from the start so that they don't get mad at you down the road for suddenly doing ad reads.

PODCAST WEBSITES

Having a home for your podcast in the form of a website is highly recommended if you plan to monetize your show. Not only does having a website help you appear more professional, it also allows you to create a separate "show notes" page for each episode. On each episode's show notes page, you can create a list of resources and links discussed in that episode. This makes it easier for your listeners to find the sponsors and resources you mentioned.

You can see an example of this on my website here: Scan the QR code or go to revolutionoilspodcast.com/revolution-podcast/how-essential-oils-work

Having a website also allows you to set up your own online store where you can sell podcast swag, products, or services. A website also allows for more listener interaction. On my podcast website, people can sign up for my newsletter, submit a favorite DIY essential oil recipe, and also check out my digital products.

Action Step:
Consider the tips about advertising, and write down which monetization strategies will work best for your launch phase as well as for your long-term goals. If you plan to create a website for your podcast, explore options like Squarespace, Wix, Weebly, or Bluehost to build it with. Remember, some media host will provide a website for you. Check to see if that will suit your needs.

"THE END IS
NEVER THE END. IT'S
ALWAYS THE BEGINNING
OF SOMETHING."

- KATE LORD BROWN

CONCLUSION

A PINEAPPLE PODCASTER

Congratulations! If you've read through the contents of this book and followed through on the action steps, then you my friend, are well on your way to becoming a Pineapple Podcaster!

Let's review what it means to be a Pineapple Podcaster:

- A Pineapple Podcaster first and foremost has a podcast idea that they are passionate about. They have an idea worth sharing that's unique and something they deem to be entertaining and of service to others.

- A Pineapple Podcaster takes time to develop their show style, format, and unique qualities. They use their creativity and insist on experimenting. They accept constructive criticism. They don't settle for boring and are willing to develop new skills to achieve their vision.

- A Pineapple Podcaster prioritizes quality. They don't settle for bad sound quality for themselves or for their guests. They outsource where needed or learn the skills required to get it done.

- A Pineapple Podcaster strives for great quality and takes the time to strategize important tactics for their show launch and growth, BUT they don't become paralyzed by perfection and are willing to compromise on certain things if it means getting the job done.

- A Pineapple Podcaster shows up for their audience. They keep their promises, stick with what they started, and don't flake out.

- A Pineapple Podcaster takes steps to actively grow their podcast by being smart about keywords and by getting in front of their target audience whenever possible.

- A Pineapple Podcaster ensures a sustainable podcast by getting paid for their efforts. They serve their audience with great content and offer relevant opportunities for listeners to support their work.

- And lastly, like our fruit brethren, a Pineapple Podcaster stands tall, wears a crown, and always stays sweet.

From the bottom of my heart, I wish you all the best success with your podcast journey. Now go out there and create something beautiful!

XO,

Samantha Lee Wright

RESOURCES

The world of podcasting is always changing. It's important to stay on top of current events and to always be developing new skills. Below are resources for ongoing education and community involvement.

Podcast Coaching with Samantha Lee Wright - Inquire about one-on-one podcast coaching at samanthaleewright.com

The Feed - A Podcast by Libsyn - Covers current events and news important to podcasters.

The Audacity to Podcast - A great podcast full of current tips and strategies for podcasters.

Podcast Guest - A newsletter that connects podcasters with guests for their shows and visa versa.

She Podcasts Facebook Group - A private educational and supportive community for female podcasters.

Follow Samantha Lee Wright:

Instagram: @samleewright
Facebook: facebook.com/lifebysamwright/
Podcast: revolutionoilspodcast.com/
Connect further at: www.samanthaleewright.com

Made in the USA
Coppell, TX
09 December 2020

43360431R00062